TALKING ABOUT
MYSELF

RACISM

Interviews by Angela Neustatter
Photographs by Laurence Cendrowicz

W
FRANKLIN WATTS
LONDON • SYDNEY

First published in 2008 by Franklin Watts

Franklin Watts,
338 Euston Road,
London, NW1 3BH

Franklin Watts Australia,
Level 17/207 Kent Street,
Sydney, NSW 2000

Copyright © Franklin Watts 2008

Series editor: Sarah Peutrill
Art Director: Jonathan Hair
Design: Elaine Wilkinson
Researcher: Charlotte Wormald
Panels written by: Sarah Ridley
Photographs: Laurence Cendrowicz (unless otherwise stated)

The Author and Publisher would like to thank the interviewees for their contributions to this book.

Picture credits: Laurence Gough/Shutterstock: 10, 11. Alex Jackson/Shutterstock: 28. Olly Hoeben 12, 13. Tomas Loutocky/Shutterstock: 14. Mypokcik/Shutterstock: 25. Zaichenko Olga/Shutterstock: 23. PhotoCreate/Shutterstock: 21. Oscar Schnell/Shutterstock: 17. Every attempt has been made to clear copyright. Should there be any inadvertent omission please apply to the publisher for rectification.

Dewey number: 305.8
ISBN: 978 0 7496 7705 3

Printed in China

Franklin Watts is a division of Hachette Children's Books,
an Hachette Livre UK company.

CONTENTS

WHAT IS RACISM?

There are a lot of misconceptions about racism. Some people believe racism only means a violent act or an attack. Others believe racism applies only to black people. There are those who think if someone has come to Britain from another country they have the right to discriminate against them.

In fact racism can be anything from name-calling, verbal abuse, threats, social exclusion and offensive graffiti to property damage and physical attack. People of all different nationalities, colours and creeds suffer racism – Africans, African-Caribbeans, Asians, Eastern Europeans and white British. People may also be racially abused because of their religion.

Why are people racist?

Unfortunately racism can exist in all races and cultures. Racists may feel threatened by anyone who is from a different race or culture. This most often affects new immigrants to a country. People who move to Britain from abroad often find themselves victims of racism, often by people who feel threatened by the country being 'flooded' with refugees. However, Britain actually takes fewer refugees than many other European countries. Austria, for example, takes more than three times as many as Britain. Sadly because racists do not usually learn about the lives and circumstances of their victims, they may not realise that they might be abusing someone who has come to Britain as a refugee to escape war, torture or death.

Racism can also be a way for racists to try to gain power and domination. The people who are on top wish to be further on top. If they cannot rise themselves, they try to achieve it by forcing others down - by harming their self-esteem for example.

Childline, the helpline for young people, which gets more than 500 calls and letters about racist bullying every year, says: "We are not born racist. Our views and beliefs develop as we grow up. If a child or young person grows up within a racist family, or has friends who are racist, they may believe it is normal and acceptable."

The effects of racism

It is not difficult to imagine the amount of distress, anger and frustration that being insulted and attacked simply because of your racial heritage can cause.

Childline is clear how damaging this is: "Racism can have a terrible effect. Children and young people can become lonely, isolated, angry and depressed. They may lose self-confidence and become terrified of going to school or going out alone."

Racism, the law and in schools

Racist incidents ranging from harassment and abuse to physical violence are against the law. Encouraging others to be racist – inciting racial hatred – is also a criminal offence.

Racist behaviour happens most often with young adolescents as both victims and perpetrators but younger children suffer it as well. In schools children can all too easily join in with racist bullying without thinking about how it would feel if they were treated this way. It is also very important that schools discuss racism as part of school life.

This book

In the interviews in this book children and young people describe their experiences of racism. Through their stories we see how painful and damaging it is when others abuse you simply because of who and what you are. The interviewees have agreed to speak out because they hope it will help others to see how cruel and ignorant racism is. In the most extreme examples, as Mully and Jasmine show, racism leads people to commit violent crimes, which often mean a prison sentence.

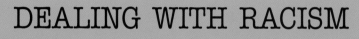

DEALING WITH RACISM

IF YOU ARE A VICTIM OF RACISM:
You don't have to accept racism. Everyone has a right to live happily and free from discrimination.

Remember you're not the one with the problem. Your self-esteem may have taken a knock but you are not the one to have caused the problem.

Think who's the best person to talk to about what's happening. Schools and the police have a responsibility to protect you. Racist bullying at school should be reported to a teacher. Many schools have anti-racist policies where they will deal with racism very firmly. If yours does not, ask your parents to ask the school about setting one up. Look at page 31 for details of organisations that you can talk to as well.

Make people take you seriously. If you are going to alert someone to the fact that you're being threatened, abused or bullied, then do it properly. You have to be prepared to get across how it is affecting you. Keeping some evidence, such as a diary, may help.

Keep safe and aware. You can't spend your life looking over your shoulder, but it pays to be aware of dangers. Stick with groups of friends if you feel vulnerable.

IF YOU SEE A FRIEND BEING A VICTIM:
Being the subject of racist abuse damages self-esteem. You can help by listening to your friend talk about their experiences – a good way to vent anger, frustration and feelings of injustice.

They may feel like no-one is taking their problem to heart. Make sure they know you take them seriously, you sympathise and are prepared to help sort out the situation.

If your friend is scared to get help, or wary of being branded 'a grass', then it might take a third party – you – to alert attention to the problem.

It's hard to make a stand, even if you're not the victim. You may be worried that you'll be next. But what you shouldn't do is join in, hoping that if you share their views you'll be safe. Report incidents to someone else who can act on your behalf if you don't want to get involved directly.

TRYING TO BELONG

Habib, 16, is Pakistani. He has grown up in an almost entirely white working class area experiencing racism. But things got much worse after 9/11 (see page 9) and he joined a criminal gang.

Q **Did you always suffer racist comments and abuse?**

No. Primary school was fine. Small children don't seem to notice that you are different. But as I became bigger people on the streets said things about 'coloureds' coming to their area and it felt horrible. When I told my parents they tried not to let it affect me. They were very protective.

" … people on the streets said things about 'coloureds' coming to their area …"

Q So when did things become harder for you?

When I went to secondary school. I was bullied a lot. Other kids took my money, commented on the colour of my skin, and called me names like Mowgli, the boy from *The Jungle Book*. It wasn't affectionate or friendly. But the teachers didn't seem to notice at all.

Q Were there other children from ethnic minorities at this school?

There were black kids but it was different for them. They seemed to be respected. I think because so many blacks are successful in music and show business and they have an identity. As a Muslim Asian I was seen very differently.

Q So what did this do to you?

It tore me apart. It really hurt. I ended up feeling completely on my own.

"... some were saying things like, 'How could you people have done that?'"

Q What made you decide you needed to react?

I went to live with my mum in London – my parents are separated – for a few months, and I went to school there. It was a really multi-cultural place and Asian kids told me I should stand up for myself. So when I went back to Kent I started fighting people when they called me names. But they just thought it a joke.

Q So how did that make you feel?

It made me very angry but I kept that inside me. Then 9/11 happened and things got a lot worse because I am Muslim and everyone seemed to be looking at me in a hostile way. On buses people eyed me and moved away from me. Everyone was talking about what had happened and some were saying things like, 'How could you people have done that?'

Q Did you react to this?

Not directly but I think it was the reason I joined a gang. I badly wanted to be somebody, not the outsider and although they were mostly whites they welcomed me in. As a gang we went out on the streets and got into fights and sometimes people were quite badly hurt. Me too. I believe the anger I dealt out reached a different level because I had all this sense of injustice inside. I never used guns or knives, although other people did, but I got picked up by the police several times. I was convicted of assault, so I have a record, which I really regret.

Q Did you see that you were on a dangerous and destructive path?

I didn't think about that until my two cousins who were also in a gang were given long prison sentences for armed robbery. Those guys were very special. They had always been there for me when my parents separated. That made me stop and really think what I was doing with my life. ▶

So where did that thinking lead?

I started wanting to do something about the gang culture and how it draws kids in because they can't see a better way. With a mate I started writing music and lyrics about this and I wrote a song about what it's like to grow up as an Asian in British society. We make discs of our songs.

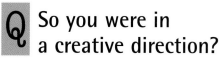 ## So you were in a creative direction?

That's how it felt. Then I came across *Oi!* – a magazine for young people in the Kent area. I asked if I could have a go at putting together their music page and they said yes.

 ## Did that make a difference to you?

Completely. Suddenly I had something valuable to do and my colour was unimportant. We were all part of a project that excited us. I wrote a big article telling my story of getting into gangs, and how it was a reaction to racism, and saying the way I chose to deal with it was wrong.

And what about now if people treat you in a racist way?

I feel worth something. My parents, whom I've caused a lot of grief, are happy with me. So if someone's racist I take no notice and just say 'whatever'. I know I won't go back on the bad road again. I've too much to do with my life. ∎

> "Suddenly I had something valuable to do and my colour was unimportant."

On September 11th, 2001, terrorists hijacked four passenger planes in the USA and deliberately crashed them. Two planes flew into the World Trade Center building in New York, which quickly collapsed. Another plane crashed into the Pentagon, Washington, the centre of US defence, and the fourth crashed to the ground. The death toll that day reached 2,973 people.

WHO DID IT?

All the hijackers obviously died in the attacks but US intelligence forces traced a link back to an organisation called Al-Qaeda. This Islamic terrorist network, led by Osama Bin Laden (originally of Saudi Arabia) seemed to have trained the hijackers.

WORLDWIDE HORROR

As pictures of the planes hitting the twin towers of the World Trade Center flashed around the world, people were stunned and terrified by what had happened. If the USA could be attacked in this way, where could they feel safe?

POLITICAL AFTERMATH

The immediate effect of the attacks, quickly named '9/11' (pronounced nine-eleven), was that US President George W Bush launched the so-called 'war on terror', with the aim of destroying the terrorist network that had planned 9/11. Believing that Osama Bin Laden, the leader of Al-Qaeda, was running training camps in Afghanistan, the US government demanded that the Afghan government, the Taleban, hand him over. When they refused to do so, US, British and anti-Taleban Afghan fighters joined forces to attack the Taleban and capture Bin Laden. By November 2001 they had toppled the Taleban government but Bin Laden escaped capture.

ANTI-MUSLIM FEELING

Since 9/11 many Muslims have reported a rise in anti-Muslim feelings. There have been physical attacks on individuals, mosques and businesses as well as a rise in racial discrimination and harassment. Trouble has grown in some areas between Muslims and their Hindu or Sikh neighbours, who have tried to distance themselves from Muslims. Many in the media (newspapers, radio and television stations) tend to focus on the actions of extreme Muslim religious leaders without saying how few Muslims actually agree with them. Generally Muslims feel upset or angry at the way they are associated with the actions of a tiny extreme minority.

CULTURE CLASH

Rosa*, 12, is from Somalia. Her family came to Britain as asylum seekers two years ago. Rosa was racially bullied at school by children of Caribbean origin, but has been helped by a peer mediator.

*Not her real name. Photo posed by model.

At primary school I worked hard and did well. The teachers liked me for that. It was a school with a lot of ethnic minorities and I had many friends.

Too shy

But I moved to secondary school and the black kids were mostly Caribbean and very lively. I'm rather shy and quiet and they didn't like me because they thought I was boring and they used to say black

"... they used to say black girls are supposed to be fun."

girls are supposed to be fun. They wanted me to do things with them that would have got us into trouble. When I refused they ganged up against me and said I was a loser. They said I had funny skin because I came from Africa and not the Caribbean.

And they didn't like it that I worked hard at my studies, and put my hand up to answer questions in class. I got texts from them calling me a smelly swot and cussing me.

I used to go home and cry in my bedroom. I told my sister, and she was nice to me, but she couldn't do anything. I didn't want to worry my parents by telling them.

Peer mediation

One day at assembly the headteacher announced that they had set up peer mediation for children having problems and it was being held at lunchtimes. I went along and there was a group of older kids sitting around a table.

I told them what was wrong and they were kind and seemed to understand. They said they would speak to the girls teasing me, and we would be asked to come together to sort it out. I was nervous about that because I thought they would treat me even worse afterwards.

We all had to sit at the table and the girls were making a fuss, saying they didn't want to be there. But the mediator got quite tough and asked each of them why they were bullying me and was there something about

me that needed sorting out. The girls didn't really have an answer to that. And then the mediators started asking if they just wanted to make me unhappy for fun, and how would they feel if it was them? I expected them to laugh or cuss, but actually one girl said she felt bad, she hadn't thought about it. And another agreed. At the end of the session the mediator asked us all to shake hands and we did.

I don't quite know why that made things better, but it did. The girls stopped teasing me and in fact one has become a friend. I'm much happier now. ■

BEING THE OUTSIDER

Florian, 14, is Dutch-French but was born in France where he lives. However, his distinctive red hair has identified him as 'different' at the rural school he attends in France.

In my first school there were children from different countries and so we were all different and the same. But when I was seven I moved to another school where the children have all grown up in that small area and they thought me strange because I am half-Dutch and I have red hair which is quite long. My family also live in a very environmentally-conscious, fairly unconventional way, which the people around here don't understand. But my mother and father have always helped me to see that being an individual can be a good thing.

> "... my mother and father have always helped me to see that being an individual can be a good thing."

Teasing

The children teased me a lot in a very personal way saying things like I was stinking, and shouting, 'Look out here is Florian. Do you have disinfectant?' The children all came from farming families who had never travelled and were very prejudiced against people from other countries. I have Dutch friends who come to stay in the holidays so that gives them more ammunition for thinking I'm an outsider.

Telling the teacher

One person wanted to be my friend and he was for a long time, but then he suddenly started being unpleasant and I saw he had joined up with the other children who were always on at me. I was very miserable at school and my mother tells me I was always hiding when she came to collect me. She

suggested I tell the teacher. I told one teacher I thought was kind, but she didn't believe me, particularly that girls would say such nasty things.

My parents tried to help, they offered me advice and on one occasion went to the teacher themselves, but nothing changed.

Over the two years when I was going into my teens I was more and more unhappy and tried to keep away from everyone in school. I never asked to join in games because I just got told I wasn't one of them if I did. Even so whenever I passed them in school they said nasty things. The teachers never intervened even though they knew I was being excluded.

Family support

There have been times when I really wanted to hit the children teasing me, and attacking me, but I knew I mustn't do that. It's got a bit easier now because I am bigger and I took up karate, which makes me feel stronger. And I am very lucky to have a family I can talk to and who are supportive and help me realise that being different isn't a bad thing. Without them I don't know how I would have coped. ■

"It's got a bit easier now because I am bigger and I took up karate, which makes me feel stronger."

ANTI-SEMITIC ATTACK

Jasmine*, 13, was the victim of an anti-Semitic racist attack and is still suffering the effects a year later.

* Photos posed by model.

Q Why do you believe your attack was racially motivated?

A friend and I got on to the bus after we had been shopping and a group of girls and boys got on afterwards. One had an Iranian boyfriend with her and I saw him say something in her ear. It was then she asked me, 'Are you Jewish?' but she didn't ask my friend who was wearing a crucifix. When she said that I felt frightened.

" ... she asked me, 'Are you Jewish?' ... I felt frightened."

Q What did you do?

I said I was English. But I went red, which I do when I am nervous. The girl saw this and stood up so she was standing over me. ▶

14

Anti-Semitism is hostility, hatred or prejudice shown towards Jews. It can take many forms: a physical attack on a person, place of worship (synagogue), cemetery, Jewish business or home; a verbal attack on Jewish culture and beliefs; systematic persecution.

WHO ARE THE JEWS?

Traditionally, everyone born of a Jewish mother is considered Jewish, whether or not they practise the religion of Judaism. Judaism goes back 4,000 years and is the oldest religion to believe in one God.

They trace their origins back to a group of people called the Hebrews who lived in what is now the Middle East.

THE BEGINNINGS OF ANTI-SEMITISM

Anti-Semitism goes back over 2,000 years, to the time of the Romans. By following their religious laws, Jews were seen to be going against the Roman government. Since then, Christians have often persecuted Jews for various reasons. The Jews have been blamed for the death of Jesus who, according to the writings of the Bible, could have been saved from crucifixion by the Jewish crowd.

PERSECUTION AND EXPULSION

During the medieval period (c. 1000¬c.1485), many Jews were persecuted in Europe. They were seen to be different because of their religion, and often became unpopular due to being involved in the money-lending business. This situation arose because Christians were forbidden by their religion to loan money and charge interest. Jews provided this service instead, especially as they were banned from other professions.

There were massacres and expulsions in England, France and Spain. In other countries, Jews were forced to live in the worst areas of a city or town, known as a ghetto. In the late 19th century, many Russian, Polish and Lithuanian Jews were massacred.

THE HOLOCAUST

Then, in the 1930s and 1940s, the Nazi Party of Germany, led by Adolf Hitler, began to systematically persecute European Jews. They wanted to rid Europe of all Jewish people. This terrible period, known as the Holocaust, led to the establishment of death camps where six million Jews were murdered.

THE MIDDLE EAST

All this persecution over the years has led to many Jews immigrating. In particular after World War I (1914–18) there was a rise in Jewish immigration to Palestine, in the Middle East, which many Jews still regarded as their own land. This led to tensions with the majority Arab population, which were further heightened when an independent Jewish state, Israel, was declared in 1948. The effect of this has been half a century of conflict between Arabs and Israelis.

ANTI-SEMITISM TODAY

Anti-Semitism continues around the world today. Many countries have laws to control anti-Semitism but it requires vigilance to ensure that these laws are followed.

Q What did you do?

I was trying to get to a place on the bus where I could get off but she came up to me and slapped me. I slapped her back and she hit me twice. I fell backwards and hit my head. Then she was pushing me and pulling my hair. I don't remember more because I went unconscious.

Q Did they also attack your friend?

No and that's why I think it was a racial attack. Why would she have asked if I was Jewish if it wasn't important? Anyway it was after her boyfriend spoke to her that the girl came over.

Q Were there other people on the bus to help you?

Yes but nobody did anything even though I was screaming and so was my friend. I can't imagine it looked like young people having fun. Perhaps people were frightened because the girl had about eight others with her. But it's terrible to think people will just watch somebody being beaten badly. In the photos taken later for the police my face was swollen and very bruised. My eyes had swelled up and were half closed. One was red and one black. Clumps of hair had been pulled out of my head.

Q So what happened then?

When the bus stopped my friend got me off. People from the houses in the street saw us and an Arab woman and a Jewish woman both rushed over to help. They called the police. I was taken to hospital.

Q Had you felt worried about being Jewish before this?

A bit since 9/11. I'm not a practising Jew but there were girls at my old school making jokes about Jewish people and there was an Arab girl who wrote anti-Semitic stuff in a book. Sometimes on the street I felt at risk.

Q Did anything happen to the girl who attacked you?

She was prosecuted and that seemed right, but going to court was horrible. The defence lawyer told me I was lying. He made me cry. But the girl was convicted and given 10 months in prison. I was happy about that, but now she is appealing and I am frightened she will come out. Also, her sister is around and I am frightened she will do something to me.

" nobody did anything even though I was screaming and so was my friend. ... it's terrible to think people will just watch ..."

> *"My moods are very up and down. I see a psychiatrist and I'm not doing well at school. I was always in the top band before but my grades have slipped down."*

 ## Has it affected your life in other ways?

My moods are very up and down. I see a psychiatrist and I'm not doing well at school. I was always in the top band before but my grades have slipped down.

 ## What are the things that have helped you?

I have been doing a course with an organisation called Streetwise that helps Jewish young people feel safe in lots of ways, including dealing with anti-Semitism. That has made me feel more able to cope. And I have a cousin I am close to and I can talk to her. She helps me to feel like I used to before the attack. And Mum and Dad have helped a lot. Even when I am being difficult with them they let me know they are there for me and understand.

> *"But still I know that I can be identified as Jewish and there are people in the world who want to hurt Jews, and how can that not be a worry?"*

 ## Do you feel this attack will have a long-term effect on you?

I think I will get over it and I can imagine being happy again, now. But still I know that I can be identified as Jewish and there are people in the world who want to hurt Jews, and how can that not be a worry? I do believe if I was Christian I would feel much safer. ■

BULLIED BY OTHER MUSLIMS

Talant, 16, came to England from Kosovo four years ago after his mother died and his father disappeared. He was at first bullied by Asian Muslims. He has won awards for his volunteer work at the school he attended.

Q **Did you come to England with other family members?**

My grandfather wanted me and my brother to come to England and make a new life but in the end I came alone. My grandfather fixed everything and all I remember is being in a lorry, always travelling at night. I didn't know where I was and I felt very frightened and unhappy.

"My grandfather wanted me and my brother to come to England and make a new life but in the end I came alone."

What happened when you reached the UK? Did you feel welcomed?

Somebody came and spoke to us and then a person from social services came and I was placed with an Indian family but that didn't work out. Now I'm with a Turkish-Cypriot family with two small children.

Are you happier with them?

They are very kind and treat me like their own child. All the same I am very aware of being different, and I don't know much about their background and they don't understand mine.

> "I didn't dare go to the canteen because they pushed me, and tried to scare me. It was the same in the playground."

Did this family put you into school?

I went to George Green's School in the East End of London. There was a group of about 20 Asian boys who called me names because I come from Kosovo even though I was Muslim too. They caused me a lot of trouble. I didn't dare go to the canteen because they pushed me, and tried to scare me. It was the same in the playground. I didn't speak English at first so I couldn't answer back.

Did other children join in?

It was only the Asian boys. The black and the white children were friendly, and one Chinese boy tried to be my protector. They were never picked on by the Asians, it was just me. ▶

Q So what did you do?

I began to feel very upset a lot of the time. And I was sad when I thought about my family in Kosovo because I know I have to forget them.

Q So how did this affect you?

I started getting into fights out of frustration and because I wanted to show that I wasn't weak or afraid of the Asian boys. But they often hurt me when they punched with their fists because they wore big rings. One day I had a bad fight and I hurt one of the boys who were calling my country bad names. We were all told we would be sent out of the school if we carried on fighting and that I must tell the teachers when I was being tormented.

Q So how did you deal with things then?

I didn't want to leave the school because it's been very

good to me. They have really helped me with my studies and they noticed when I was unhappy.

Q What happened after this?

It all got easier as I learned to speak English. It took about a year. I think I seemed particularly strange and different because all the other children, whatever their race, spoke English. I worked hard to learn. I went to classes after school and I looked in the dictionary every time I needed a word.

Q What has been most important in helping you feel you belong in England?

It was becoming a volunteer. I used to play football at school lunchtimes and when there was an open evening I saw information for CSV (Community Service Volunteers) asking for people to help run activities for younger children in the summer school holidays. My foster mother suggested this would be good for me so I applied and was accepted. On the football pitches

RACISM IN FOOTBALL

Many people, like Talant, find that sports such as football are a great way to break down differences. However even the beautiful game suffers from racism. In football, racism is a world-wide phenomenon particularly in Italy, Spain and Eastern Europe. Racism isn't directed at players simply because of their skin colour; players are also targeted because of their nationality, religion or ethnicity. Some players may be targeted by supporters more because they play for an opposing team rather than their appearance. However, some players have been targeted even by their own fans.

In response to this, 'Kick It Out', football's anti-racism campaign, was launched in 1993. Their work includes professional football education for young people, tackling racial abuse and harassment in park football and raising the issue of the exclusion of south Asians as professional footballers from the game.

> "On the football pitches every day I made more friends, and I saw that people really liked and admired me."

Photo posed by models.

every day I made more friends, and I saw that people really liked and admired me. That made me a lot happier and I didn't feel the need to be so angry any more. After I had finished my GCSEs this year I did more volunteering helping co-ordinate a sports festival and I'm part of the Positive Playgrounds Team and every lunchtime I'm in the playground making sure the kids don't get into fights. Now I see the younger pupils look up to me and that feels good.

Q So volunteering has been very important for you?

Definitely. I won the Good Citizen Award for my CSV work and I was a runner up for the Princess Diana Award. I have met other Kosovans but I don't want to belong with them. I want to be recognised as British.

BREAKING DOWN RACISM

Mully, 15, came to the UK from the Congo, with his family, aged four. He has suffered some serious racism and wants to break down racism among children through a school club.

I've experienced a little bit of racism at school. Like when white kids told me I couldn't join in football because I was black. And there was a white girl who wanted to go out with me but she said her parents would never let her go out with a black boy. But my mum used to tell me that, as Christians, we are all the same, and not to take any notice.

Attacked

It was outside school that the really bad racism happened and that made me very frightened. I saw how much some people hate blacks. I had gone to Romford in Essex to visit a friend but as I was getting off the bus a bunch of white young men came out of the pub and said: 'No blacks here.'

I managed to get off the bus and my friend who is also black, was there to meet me. I said we should run and hide. Then the whites got into cars and on to bikes and

came after us. I hid in a bush and tried to call the police but they saw me and as I ran they tripped me up so I fell. They hit me with a bottle on my head. I passed out but a white man saw me and called the police. When they arrived I was dizzy and being sick and I had a cut on my face. I had lumps on my head.

Moving on

My mum was very upset and worries when I go out. Dad was very angry but he says the important thing is for me to do the best I can educationally and prove I'm a worthwhile person in the world. That way I can beat ignorant racists.

I felt scared after the attack but I have been picked to play football for Charlton FC for their junior team and that feels really good because there I belong among the white kids.

At my school people from the LEAP programme, which teaches conflict resolution, came to do training with some children and I was chosen. Since then I, and some others who are trained, have set up a club where children can come to talk about problems they have with other children and we try to sort these out. I particularly want to be able to sort out racial conflicts. If I can be someone children look up to then perhaps I can help to break down racism. ■

"I particularly want to be able to sort out racial conflicts. If I can be someone children look up to then perhaps I can help to break down racism."

NOT ALLOWED TO MIX

Michelle, 19, was a victim of white-on-white racism at school and because of this, left early. It took an unusual therapy to help her.

Q **Growing up did you mix with different races?**

Four of my uncles married black women so I've always seen them as part of my world. At primary school I had all kinds of friends and my parents' attitude is that we are all human and it's how we behave not our race that matters.

"At primary school I had all kinds of friends and my parents' attitude is that we are all human and it's how we behave not our race that matters."

> *"One day in science they pinned one of my black friends on to the floor, then poured acid from a glass tube, which we were using for an experiment, on to her arm."*

 So when did you begin to have problems with other pupils?

At secondary school. We lived in a very white area outside Bristol. But at school there was a bunch of black girls and I liked hanging out with them although I had white friends too. There was a group of white girls at school who really didn't like blacks and they saw me as a traitor for mixing with them and wearing my hair in braids.

So did this group of girls bother you?

Yes. One of the girls had a skinhead dad who used to come to school and shout at the headteacher that black children shouldn't be admitted.

So how did these girls treat you?

They tried to intimidate me. They called me 'wigger' and shouted abuse at me. They would try to trip me up or hurt me in break-times. One day, when I was walking home from school, about eight of them ran out and pushed me over. They had a bucket of black paint and they pushed my face into it shouting, 'If you want to be a black, you can be.'

Was it just you they treated in this racist way?

No. They were terrible to the black girls, too. One day in science they pinned one of my black friends on to the floor, then poured acid from a glass tube, which we were using for an experiment, on to her arm. Now she has big pale patches where the skin was burnt. ▶

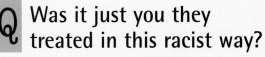

Did you report these girls to the teachers?

I tried but the school didn't do anything.
I never felt I'd get protection from them. My mother went into school several times but that didn't help either. It made me very miserable and I dreaded going to school.

 So what happened then?

My mum took me out of school just before I turned 15. I didn't want to stop my education but I couldn't cope with school.

STATISTICS ON RACIST ATTACKS

According to The British Crime Survey in 2004, 87,000 people from black or minority ethnic communities said they had been a victim of a racially motivated crime. They had suffered 49,000 violent attacks, with 4,000 being wounded.

At the same time 92,000 white people said they had also fallen victim to a racially motivated crime. The number of violent attacks against whites reached 77,000. The number of white people who reported being wounded was five times the number of black and minority ethnic victims at 20,000. Most of the offenders (57%) in the racially motivated crimes are not white. White victims said 82% of offenders were not white.

How were you feeling inside?

I felt very depressed but there was also a lot of anger. I suppose it was this that led me to get into a fight with a girl and I ended up in trouble with the police. They said I must go to college to do some vocational training, so I did that. At the same time I was getting comfort from listening to music, which I love, and I have decks so I spent a lot of time playing them.

So was college a better experience than school?

I enjoyed it and there was a counsellor there, Pamela Woodford. I went to her because my moods were so up and down. We talked about all that had happened and my life.

Did that help?

It was a relief to be able to talk about things. Then she suggested me for a special session at a place called Mindfields College where they use something called the Human Givens wind back therapy.

Did you find the therapy helpful?

It was something quite new for me. I was in a room with a lot of people. I was put into a kind of sleep-trance. I was aware of the voice of the therapist and I was talking, but as though in a dream. Joe Griffin, the therapist, got me to re-run my life, going back over the things at school that had hurt, and were still bothering me. This lasted about 45 minutes.

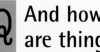

"And when I saw the girls in town they didn't bother me. I just thought they were sad."

Was there more to the therapy?

No. That was all. But it was extraordinary because all the anger and pain of what had happened went. I found in the days after that I could remember and not feel bothered. I even laughed at the pain incident. And when I saw the girls in town they didn't bother me. I just thought they were sad.

And how are things now?

I am applying to college to do the GCSEs I missed out on by leaving school early. I realise that I need these to get a job, and I realise that to really beat those girls I need to get the education I missed because of them. ∎

GROWING UP WITH RACISM

Andy*, 19, grew up in an all-Protestant area of Belfast where Catholics were the enemy. Working with a dance project has changed his feelings.

*Photo posed by model.

I lived on one of the biggest estates in Europe and I only mixed with Protestants at school and socially. Even though Catholics lived in the next street we were never friends. There were fights and knifings. My family didn't talk about why Protestants and Catholics don't get on. I just grew up hearing stories and knowing Catholics were a bad lot.

Getting into trouble

Things started going wrong in my life after my dad died when I was ten. My mum was in a dreadful state, my sister too, and we couldn't comfort each other. I bunked off school and hung out with mates on the street. I started using too much alcohol and weed.

Learning to dance

But in the end getting into difficulties did me a favour. I was sent to a behavioural unit and I agreed to go on a programme called 'Education Other Than At School', where I did pretty basic schoolwork.

"I just grew up hearing stories and knowing Catholics were a bad lot."

Then one day this woman, Mags Byrne, from an organisation called Dance United Northern Ireland came to do a project and I thought, 'Oh yeah – I'm not doing no dance!' But Mags told us this wasn't effeminate or anything; she just asked us to give it a try. It was very physical which I enjoyed and then Mags persuaded me to join a five-week project with a performance at the end. I did it because she really seemed to feel I was worth it and not many people seem to have felt that in my life. My friends slaughtered me, calling me 'Andy the Dancing Queen' but I wasn't going to be put off.

Meeting Catholics

The programme was part of something called Building Bridges where Dance United Northern Ireland work with children with difficulties, in Catholic and Protestant schools, and then get them to perform together. The idea is to break down the prejudice that's been there for so long. If I'd known this I probably would not have done it. I remember on the first project talking to this guy Kieran and realising he was from a Catholic area and after a couple of weeks it struck me he was no different to me. I never thought I'd have a Catholic mate, but it feels good. ■

NORTHERN IRELAND

For centuries, Ireland was ruled by Great Britain. Many Irish resented this and there were rebellions and plots to gain independence. In the early 20th century, the British government began to discuss ways to give the Irish independence. This happened in 1922 when 26 counties of Ireland became the Irish Free State. This left six counties in the north (Northern Ireland) where the largely Protestant population preferred British rule. In 1949 the Irish Free State became the Republic of Ireland.

RELIGION AND POLITICS

In Northern Ireland, the community is divided roughly along religious lines, even though they are all Christians. Protestants generally support the two main Unionist parties, who want to keep Northern Ireland as part of the UK. Many Catholics support the Nationalist cause as they want Northern Ireland to become part of the Republic. Catholics have often experienced discrimination such as poorer housing, schools and job opportunities.

VIOLENCE

There were many disagreements between the Protestant and Catholic communities, some of which were violent. During the 1960s this violence reached new heights. There were shootings, bombings and intimidation. In 1969 the British government sent in the army. Over the next 30 years armed groups on both sides caused more than 3,000 deaths.

GOOD FRIDAY AGREEMENT

Politicians sought solutions but there was much mistrust. Finally, in 1998, the Good Friday Agreement was signed, with the idea of setting up a devolved government with both Nationalists and Unionists. By 2002, this broke down and more years of unrest followed. A new agreement was reached in 2006. In May 2007, devolved government began with politicians working together to rule the country as part of the UK. There is still much work needed to build relationships between the religious communities.

GLOSSARY

Anti-Semitism
Anti-Semitism is hostility, hatred or prejudice shown towards Jews (see page 15).

Catholic
A member of the Roman Catholic Church, the largest group within Christianity. Catholics acknowledge the authority of the bishop of Rome, the Pope, in matters of faith.

Christian
A person who follows the teachings of Jesus Christ.

crucifix
The cross that has become the main symbol of Christianity (see crucifixion).

crucifixion
An ancient method of execution, in which the victim was tied or nailed to a large wooden cross and left to hang there until dead. Crucifixion was the method used by the Romans to put Jesus to death, and the cross has become the main Christian symbol.

devolved
A devolved government is one that has had its powers passed on from another group.

discrimination
Unfair treatment of a person or group on the basis of prejudice.

effeminate
When a male shows 'female' charactersitics, such as softness, delicacy or weakness, which contradicts traditional male gender roles.

ghetto
An often walled quarter in a European city to which Jews were restricted, beginning in the Middle Ages.

harassment
Words, conduct or action, usually repeated or persistent that causes annoyance, alarm or emotional distress to the person it is directed at.

Islamic
Muslim: of or relating to or supporting the religion of Islam.

Middle East
An area comprising the countries of southwest Asia and northeast Africa. In the 21st century the region has been the continuing scene of political and economic turmoil.

minority
A group of people who differ racially from a larger group of which it is a part.

Muslim
A follower of the religion of Islam.

persecution
The act of oppressing someone with ill-treatment, especially because of race, religion, gender, sexual orientation or beliefs.

Protestant
A name for those Christians and churches that separated from the Roman Catholic Church after 1517.

psychiatrist
A medical doctor who specialises in the diagnosis and treatment of mental disorders.

racism
When a person acts as if a person or group is inferior because of their colour, ethnicity or religion.

vigilance
The act of watching for something to happen, particularly watching for danger.

weed
A street term for the illegal drug cannabis.

FURTHER INFORMATION

ORGANISATIONS & HELPLINES

Bullying Online
Web: www.bullying.co.uk
Email: help@bullying.co.uk
Bullying Online is the UK's leading anti-bullying charity and provides support for families, individuals, schools and youth organisations. The website holds lots of information, or you can email them with further queries.

ChildLine
Free helpline: 0800 1111
Web: www.childline.org.uk
Telephone counselling for any child with any problem. If there's something bad that's happening and you want to know what to do, you can talk to them. No one else has to know anything.

Dance United Northern Ireland
Web: www.dance-united.com/workni.htm
Tel: 02890 423 552
Email: infoNI@dance-united.com
Dance United works with young people with special needs, as well as teenagers who find themselves outside of mainstream education.

LPC (Leap Confronting Conflict)
Tel: 020 7561 3700
Web: www.leaplinx.com
A national voluntary youth organisation that provides opportunities, regionally and nationally, for young people and adults to explore creative approaches to conflicts in their lives.

Streetwise
Tel: 020 78457 2331
Web: www.streetwisegb.org
Streetwise works with schools and organisations focusing on the safety and development of young Jewish people.

The Lantern Project
Web: www.lanternproject.org.uk
Supports victims of childhood abuse, domestic violence, racial abuse and bullying. Their website has extended information on racial bullying, or you can email them through the website.

There4me
Web: www.there4me.com
Helps 12-16 year olds who are worried about something and need help. They help with loads of issues including bullying. The site includes the facility to email an agony aunt for help.

Youth Access
Helpline: 020 8896 3675
Web: www.youthaccess.org.uk
Counselling services for young people aged 12–25 years.

Youth2Youth
Helpline telephone: 020 8896 3675
Web: www.youth2youth.co.uk
Support for under 19s run by young volunteers. As well as the telephone helpline, you can email them through the website.

FURTHER WEBSITES

Anti-Racist Alliance
Web: www.antiracistalliance.org.uk
This trust challenges racism by education through seminars, training, projects and publications; by supporting people subject to racism; and by offering them opportunities for training and work experience.

Kick It Out
Web: www.kickitout.org
Kick It Out works throughout the football, educational and community sectors to challenge racism and work for positive change.

Working Group Against Racism in Children's Resources
Web: www.wgarcr.org.uk
This organisation was set up to raise awareness that racism is damaging to young children and to identify anti-racist play and learning resources. They give training and information to professionals working with children.

AUSTRALIA/NEW ZEALAND

www.kidshelp.com.au
Free helpline: 1800 55 1800
Telephone and online counselling for young people under 25.

www.youthline.co.nz
Support for young people in New Zealand.

INDEX

TALKING POINTS

The interviews in this book may provoke a range of reactions: shock, sympathy, empathy, sadness. As many of the interviewees found, talking can help you to sort out your emotions. If you wish to talk about the interviews here are some questions to get you started.

Habib's story – page 6
Habib reports a change in attitude towards him since 9/11. How can individuals, groups and governments work to reverse this trend? What do you think are the main issues growing up as an Asian in British society?

Rosa's story – page 10
Rosa is bullied by other black girls, but they remark on the colour of her skin. Are they being racist? Is this kind of bullying common?

Florian's story – page 12
Why do you think people are often hostile towards 'outsiders' as they were to Florian?

Jasmine's story – page 14
Why do you think no one intervened in the attack on Jasmine? What would you do in this situation?

Talant's story – page 18
Why do you think the other Muslims picked on Talant? Why do you think volunteering helped him?

Mully's story – page 22
Mully's dad advises that the best way to deal with racism is to prove yourself educationally. Do you agree?

Michelle's story – page 24
At Michelle's school there were groups of black friends and white friends and not much mixing. Why do you think this is?

Andy's story – page 28
Andy grew up being taught racist views by his family. How easy do you think these are to lose? What other sorts of projects might work as well as Dance United did for Andy?